G000137853

Seascape

A play

Tony Rushforth

Samuel French—London
www.samuelfrench-london.co.uk

© 2007 BY TONY RUSHFORTH

Rights of Performance by Amateurs are controlled by Samuel French Ltd, 52 Fitzroy Street, London W1T 5JR, and they, or their authorized agents, issue licences to amateurs on payment of a fee. **It is an infringement of the Copyright to give any performance or public reading of the play before the fee has been paid and the licence issued.**

The Royalty Fee indicated below is subject to contract and subject to variation at the sole discretion of Samuel French Ltd.

Basic fee for each and every
performance by amateurs   Code D
in the British Isles

The publication of this play does not imply that it is necessarily available for performance by amateurs or professionals, either in the British Isles or Overseas. Amateurs and professionals considering a production are strongly advised in their own interests to apply to the appropriate agents for written consent before starting rehearsals or booking a theatre or hall.

ISBN 978 0 573 02382 8

The right of Tony Rushforth to be identified as author of this work has been asserted by him in accordance with Section 77 of the Copyright, Designs and Patents Act 1988

Please see page iv for further copyright information

SEASCAPE

An earlier version of the play was performed by The Largs Players for the Scottish Community Drama Association Festival where it reached the Scottish Finals at the Palace Theatre, Kilmarnock, on 20th April 2003. A revised version was first performed at The Questors Theatre, Ealing, on 2nd November 2005, with the following cast:

Mary	Zoe Mortimer
Hans	Tom Piccin
Magda	Maria Brusa
Kurt	Tony Barber

Directed by Tony Rushforth
Set design by Bron Blake and Jenny Richardson

COPYRIGHT INFORMATION
(See also page ii)

This play is fully protected under the Copyright Laws of the British Commonwealth of Nations, the United States of America and all countries of the Berne and Universal Copyright Conventions.

All rights, including Stage, Motion Picture, Radio, Television, Public Reading, and Translation into Foreign Languages, are strictly reserved.

No part of this publication may lawfully be reproduced in ANY form or by any means — photocopying, typescript, recording (including video-recording), manuscript, electronic, mechanical, or otherwise — or be transmitted or stored in a retrieval system, without prior permission.

Licences are issued subject to the understanding that it shall be made clear in all advertising matter that the audience will witness an amateur performance; that the names of the authors of the plays shall be included on all announcements and on all programmes; and that the integrity of the authors' work will be preserved.

The Royalty Fee is subject to contract and subject to variation at the sole discretion of Samuel French Ltd.

In Theatres or Halls seating Four Hundred or more the fee will be subject to negotiation.

In Territories Overseas the fee quoted in this Acting Edition may not apply. A fee will be quoted on application to our local authorized agent, or if there is no such agent, on application to Samuel French Ltd, London.

VIDEO-RECORDING OF AMATEUR PRODUCTIONS

Please note that the copyright laws governing video-recording are extremely complex and that it should not be assumed that any play may be video-recorded for *whatever purpose* without first obtaining the permission of the appropriate agents. The fact that a play is published by Samuel French Ltd does not indicate that video rights are available or that Samuel French Ltd controls such rights.

CHARACTERS

Mary, nearly 17
Hans, nearly 17
Magda, late 30s
Kurt, late 50s

The action of the play takes place in Port Erin on the
Isle of Man

Time—Summer 1940

PRODUCTION NOTES

The play is set on a cliff that overlooks the coast and part of the harbour. There is a small, weather-beaten bench with backrest and arms which is set on some old stone flags. A section of high barbed-wire fencing would make a significant statement.

Entrances from the town are from an upper path which should be slightly raised and there is another entrance from a lower, more precipitous path to the beach which is suggested by an angled fence.

There is a raised grass mound surrounded by pebbles and nearby are the remains of a fire.

It is important that the scenes virtually overlap, and we must be aware of the sound of the sea and the persistent screech of the seagulls discreetly fading in and out of the production.

For Jonathan and Bruno

SEASCAPE

Scene 1

A cliff top overlooking Port Erin harbour. Summer 1940

The Lights come up on Mary who is kneeling on the grass mound with her sketchbook and pencil. She is attractive and approaching seventeen and one is aware that she is now a young woman and not a girl. She is barefoot and dressed in a traditional, late 1930s, cotton summer dress which has been chosen by her mother, but Mary has belted it in such a way that it discreetly shows off her figure

Mary It was in the local paper … That was the first that we'd heard about it and the very next day they started putting up the barbed-wire fences ... with a big gate, right across the road just up from the railway station. (*She pauses*) We were told that the internees that were coming would be women, children or old men … well, that's what they said. By the end of the week we'd been given passes — identification cards. The big surprise was they weren't going to build a separate camp ... huts, sentry boxes and so on… Port Erin was to be the camp. It was difficult to take that in. (*She pauses*) A Commandant, a woman, had overall responsibility, one got used to seeing her about the town. What was amazing was that over the next months the population doubled and four thousand internees had to be accommodated ... here, in the town and they were to live in the boarding houses and hotels ... with the landladies in charge. They were free to use the town, to wander around just as if they lived here. At first it was very strange, you know, living with them ... the enemy, cheek by jowl as it were. (*She pauses*) It was the Germans who came first. (*She picks up her sketching pad and pencil and settles down to draw the distant view*)

The silence is broken by the screeching of seagulls

Hans appears from us. *He is an engaging, intelligent young man, not quite seventeen, with all the vitality and promise of youth. He notices Mary drawing and sits on the grass some distance away from her*

Mary is suddenly aware of his presence and eventually cannot resist looking up. Hans smiles at her but Mary does not know how to handle this exchange and returns to her drawing

Hans Terrific view. (*He pauses*) Don't you think so?
Mary (*excited yet shy*) Yes — yes, it is. (*Back to her drawing*)
Hans Almost surrounded by the sea.
Mary When the tide's in.
Hans Is this one of your favourite places?

Mary looks at him and nods and goes back to her drawing

Where you come and draw?
Mary It's — it's my special place … at the weekend. Not just for drawing … to get away.
Hans At home I had a special place. Like here, high up.
Mary Overlooking the sea?
Hans No. The reservoir. I used to cycle there.
Mary We have a bike and share it … it's ridiculous.
Hans Why?
Mary Because I have brothers and sisters … there's a lot of arguing… (*she smiles*) and fighting.
Hans So that's why you want to get away.

Mary nods and goes back to her drawing. Hans sees a feather on the ground and picks it up to cover that his focus is very much on Mary

Pause

Have you always lived here?

Mary No. We came for a holiday last August and stayed … because
of …

Hans Because of the war?

Mary Daddy didn't want us to go back to Sheffield.

Hans Thought there would be bombing?

Mary Yes. But Daddy went back.

Pause. Mary returns to her drawing

Hans Go to school here?

Mary (*nodding*) Buchan's Girls' School. I'm not a boarder… I go
on the train.

Hans Where to?

Mary Castletown. It's on the way to Douglas.

Hans That's where we docked. Surrounded by barbed wire … and all
down the promenade.

Mary It's everywhere. I hate it. (*She returns to her drawing*)

Hans You miss him?

Mary looks up

Your father?

Mary With Daddy it's always treats. Perhaps it's the treats I miss …
That sounds awful.

Hans No. We all like treats. (*He takes out a bag of sweets from his
pocket*) They've run out of cigarettes at the shop. Would you like a
sweet?

Mary No … No, thanks.

Hans Please. I haven't used up all my coupons.

Mary Well … all right … thank you. (*She takes a sweet*) I'm not
supposed to … to speak…

Hans To the internees?

Mary Because you're German … because of Hitler and the war. There's
a poster at the station: "Careless Talk Costs Lives".

Hans And you think you've been talking "carelessly"?

Mary No—no, of course not.

Hans Then there can't be any harm. Can there?

Mary You don't sound German…

Hans Why should I? I've never lived there. My father was born in Germany and so they've put him in the big camp … in Douglas … They wouldn't let me join him even though I'm nearly seventeen. They said, "There are documents to be consulted … about your father's — er — contacts". Suspicious bastards … Sorry.

Mary Perhaps they'll let you join him on your birthday?

Hans I just don't know.

Mary When is it?

Hans At the end of the month.

Mary It'll soon pass. And your mother?

Hans She died three years ago.

Mary I'm sorry. (*She returns to her drawing*)

Hans wanders over to the remains of a fire

Hans Someone's been lighting a fire.

Mary It's been there for months … You're not allowed to do it any more.

Hans looks at her

To light a fire on the cliffs — or on the beach. And not just because of the black-out.

Hans (*with a German accent*) Ah — ah! Of course. Smoke signals to the Germans.

Mary (*laughing*) Don't be ridiculous.

Hans Not so ridiculous. (*Confidentially*) Dad says there are German spies in Ireland — in the Free State.

Mary (*teasing*) Careless talk?

Hans (*smiling*) Don't report me.

Mary I won't.

Mary returns to her drawing and Hans throws away the feather

Hans Can I look?

Mary I'm not very good.
Hans Please.
Mary All right.

Hans crosses over and she passes him the sketchbook. He looks at the drawing and then looks up at the view

Hans It's very good. Very good.

Mary is pleased but embarrassed and Hans wants to impress her

   I like the way you've got the perspective … The seagulls in the fore-
   ground … take my eye down to the harbour … to the focus.

Mary Focus?

Hans On the boat. (*He points*) The terracotta boat … to the right of
   the jetty. You should paint it, it's a lovely colour. I can't make out
   its name…

Mary It's the *Glee Maiden*. It's Daddy's boat.

Hans Really. Then paint it — for him.

Mary (*exasperated*) I haven't any paints … I've used them all up…
   You can't buy them now because of the war.

Hans (*picking up her tone*) Do you think I've forgotten? (*He takes a
   card out of his pocket and shows her*) Hans Reinhardt … German
   Internee: Two-five-six-seven-four; and before we were shipped over
   here Father had four weeks in Strangeways.

Mary doesn't understand

   The prison… (*Sending up*) "Detained at His Majesty's pleasure".

Mary Why?

Hans Dad said they think of him as an alien — possibly a German
   spy. It's so bloody stupid. (*He passes back the sketchbook to Mary
   and moves away from her*)

Pause

Mary Sorry…

Hans (*now calm*) So am I.

Mary Where are you staying?

Hans (*smiling*) Billeted?

Mary Billeted.

Hans Well … it sounds wonderful … but it isn't. The Golf Links Hotel … in the attic … very small … and at the moment very hot … and tomorrow I've got to share with some old German chap. Can you imagine?

Mary (*excitedly*) We live in the annexe.

Hans looks at her

To The Golf Links Hotel. It's further down the road. They're letting us stay on … indefinitely. Well, as long as ——

Hans — as long as the war goes on.

Mary I haven't seen you around.

Hans I've only been here two days … it seems like weeks. Anyway, there'll be time to do some drawing … and painting. You can borrow my paints … water colours (*dramatizing*) and paint the boat terracotta.

Mary I've never used water colour. There's a special technique… I would be frightened to try.

Hans It's not so difficult … really.

There is a woman calling out from some distance away: "Coo-eee… Coo-eee…"

Mary That's Mother. I'll have to go.

Hans Can I bring them round? To your house? The paints?

Mary No. I don't think you should.

Hans But I could give you a painting lesson. Would you like me to?

Voice off stage: "Mary… Mary…"

Mary I'll see.

Mary starts to exit and stops on Hans's next line

Hans Tomorrow then? After lunch? At the hotel? We could go in the
conservatory, nobody uses it — and the light's good.

Mary Perhaps …

Hans Please.

Mary I'll try …

Hans That'll be great. (*He quickly puts his hands on her shoulder and
lightly kisses her cheek*)

*Mary is for a moment frozen to the spot and she then turns and runs
very quickly out of sight*

*Hans watches her go and in a moment responds with a buoyant
expansive waving of both arms. He then swiftly swings round and calls
out to the sky*

She stopped and waved! Yes! Yes! And she's called Mary!

*The seagulls respond loudly to his exuberance as the Lights quickly
fade to Black-out*

SCENE 2

The same

*Magda is standing near the mound, taking in the view. She is a striking,
attractive woman in her late thirties and has dark hair. She is wearing
a colourful summer dress, sandals and sunglasses. Her make-up is
discreet. She speaks with a slight Lancashire accent. She is carrying
a shopping basket which contains a thermos flask and a knitting bag.
She changes the direction of her focus and now looks down and takes
in the view of the harbour*

Magda *Non è mica male…* (*She takes off her sunglasses*) *Non è mica
male…* After the Germans it was our turn to come to the island. The
moment Italy joined forces with Germany … they were on to us. The
papers were full of it, pictures of Il Duce and Hitler… "another risk

of Fifth Column". The next day they picked me up… (*she smiles*)
literally … took me off to the station and, strange as it may seem,
this was the first time I'd been in a Black Maria. Of course I'd had
warnings from the cops but in Piccadilly that's to be expected — one
of the nightly hazards. (*Confidentially*) Before the war, I was never
— you know — on the street … no way … always tried to be with a
better class of person — had an arrangement with the doorman at the
Midland Hotel. But once war started there was concern because "big
wig officers" stayed there and they thought we were … a "security
risk"… (*She smiles*) Shades of Mata Hari. (*She pauses. During the
following, she goes to the bench and sits*) Anyway, police put me on
the boat and I caught up with Lili and some of the others. When we
arrived here we asked the Commandant to keep quiet — warned her
that if the news got out she'd have a riot on her hands. (*She takes out
her knitting*) I have toned down the make-up a little … so this is the
new, domestic image. And I enjoy it — knitting, sewing … anyway,
what else is there to do? (*She is suddenly aware of the strong sun and
puts on her sunglasses and continues to knit*)

*In a moment Kurt enters from the beach, somewhat out of breath,
wearing a tastefully coloured shirt, casual slacks and sandals. He is
a handsome man with grey hair. He is in his late fifties and speaks
with a German accent*

*Magda sees him and smiles. Kurt smiles back at her and she returns
to her knitting*

Kurt (*leaning on the fence*) It's quite a climb. I shouldn't have come
up this way — *gefährlich*.
Magda Yes. But it's worth it, and on a day like this.
Kurt Have you been here long?

Magda looks at him

   I mean on the island.
Magda I arrived yesterday. And you?

Kurt Last week.

Magda (*taking off her sunglasses*) Well, then … you can tell me all about it. About *la vita*… I mean "life" on the island.

Kurt About life in Port Erin. We're not given the chance to know about life on the island. That is … if … you are…? ·

Magda (*laughing*) An internee … of course.

Kurt Of course. It was silly of me to think that you'd come here from choice.

Magda *Grazie!* (*She laughs*) *Grazie!* Join the masses on their wake's week in Douglas? Fit in the T.T. races? No, no. Not exactly my *scena* — er — "scene".

Kurt And what, may I ask is your … scene? Lake Garda? Sorrento? Florence?

Magda Actually my mother came from Como and she did take me back while her parents were alive … when I was a teenager … a long time ago.

Kurt Come now. Not so long as all that.

Magda How very … chivalrous. However it was a very long time ago.

Kurt If you insist. Are you bilingual?

Magda Had to be. Mother never learned English.

Kurt It can't have been easy.

Magda No. No, it wasn't. (*She returns to her knitting*)

Pause

Kurt moves further DS and looks down towards the harbour

Kurt Not many boats down there.

Magda No.

Kurt Two of the big ones were lost, when they went to the rescue.

Magda Rescue?

Kurt Dunkirk.

Magda Of course. Like the Pied Piper … all those soldiers — drawn into the sea.

Kurt A sitting target. History repeating itself. (*He pauses*) And they've taken over Norway.

Magda They're getting nearer.

Kurt Last week an internee, who had been forcibly separated from her husband, took one of the rowing boats in the middle of the night. The boat capsized and she drowned.

Magda Poor woman.

Kurt Desperate woman… (*He pauses*) The boats that are left go out regularly … you'll find that the diet is principally fish … but at least it's fresh. I have to take my turn doing the cooking once a week.

Magda Where?

Kurt The Golf Links Hotel.

Magda Lucky you.

Kurt Believe me, it's no Grand Hotel … in the Vicki Baum sense.

Magda I loved the film.

Kurt Well … anything with Garbo.

Magda Well … anything with Barrymore…

They laugh

Kurt (*taking out a cheroot*) Would you like one?

Magda No, thanks.

Kurt Where are you staying?

Magda A boarding house … in the town. Very bleak, overcrowded, and I suspect in winter, very cold.

Kurt Do you expect to stay on?

Magda Unless I can make the authorities realize that I'm not a fascist… Are you … are you a Nazi?

Kurt That's very direct.

Magda I like to know where I stand. I like to call a spade a spade … are you?

Kurt How could I be… I'm Jewish.

Magda I see. Your English is very good.

Kurt Thank you. I studied it for a while at university.

Magda And how long have you lived in England?

Kurt Six years … The writing was on the wall, but my friends in Berlin wouldn't listen to me. Some escaped at the last minute and told me what's happening … what the Nazis are doing … the *rassentrennung…*

Magda looks at him

I mean the segregation … confiscating possessions … setting up special camps. Thousands of people are disappearing … on special trains … and anytime now it will happen in Italy.

Magda The Italians wouldn't allow it.

Kurt You'll see. Il Duce will have to toe Hitler's party line and a lot of people will use this to settle old scores. Even here in the hotel, there's a real split between the Jewish and pro-Nazi women. The authorities shouldn't be so stupid, they shouldn't mix us up like this under the same roof … it's asking for trouble.

Magda I don't know how the land lies in my place … it's early days, everyone's being very cagey. In any case, I'm deliberately keeping a low profile.

Kurt Why? What have you got to hide?

Magda I … I don't want to talk about it.

Kurt I'm sorry. It's none of my business. Forgive me.

Magda takes a small thermos flask and a cup out of her basket

Magda Would you like to have a cup of real coffee? I smuggled it over … it won't last for long.

Kurt (*sitting on the bench*) Oh … that would be marvellous … you'll find that here they only have tea. Strong, stewed tea.

Magda pours out the coffee

Magda I know … it's just like the tea at Piccadilly…

Kurt The underground?

Magda No … No… Manchester … the railway station.

Kurt Is that where you live?

Magda Yes. I haven't brought any milk and, of course, there's no sugar.

Kurt That's fine. I like it black.

Magda I brought a spare cup in case my friend Lili came up, but she must have gone for her swim.

Kurt She's very brave.

Magda I know but she wants to keep her figure to … to keep fit.

They both enjoy the coffee

Kurt This is delicious … thank you.

Magda My pleasure.

Kurt May I ask what you do … did … in Manchester?

Magda Do you know the city?

Kurt Reasonably well. I used to come up … because of my work … from time to time…

Magda Your work?

Kurt I'm a designer, for the theatre and a number of our shows have opened there.

Magda What kind of shows?

Kurt Musical comedies, revues, usually at the Opera House … sometimes at the Palace … then they go on tour before … hopefully opening in the West End.

Magda I'm not surprised that you're in show business… I thought there was … something about you.

Kurt (*laughing*) I hope that my manner isn't … too theatrical? Or do you mean effeminate?

Magda Oh, no … no. Not at all. Believe me, I can tell the difference between a … no … it's just that you're … oh … now you've embarrassed me.

Kurt Tell me.

Magda You've got style … that's it. Style. You're a gentleman.

Kurt Thank you.

Pause. He takes her hand

What a nice thing to say.

After a moment Magda withdraws her hand and looks at her watch

Magda I'll have to go. (*She puts the thermos flask and the cups in the basket and rises*) Mrs Parker, our landlady, is holding a meeting … setting up the work rotas … all very exciting.

Kurt (*rising*) Then you mustn't be late. (*He smiles*) It's worth keeping on the right side of your landlady … believe me. They report to the Commandant.

Magda A kind of secret service?

Kurt Maybe.

Magda (*dramatizing*) *The Lady Vanishes*? (*She laughs*)

Kurt It's not quite like that. You've seen too many films. I'll walk back with you.

Magda No … thanks… I'd rather go on my own … Goodbye. (*She starts to move to the beach path*)

Kurt Take the top path, it's safer. (*He notices Magda's knitting and picks it up from the ground*) Don't forget your knitting.

Magda stops and turns

Magda Thanks.

Kurt Can I see you tomorrow? (*He pauses*) Please.

Magda It just depends …

Kurt I'd like to talk to you … to hear about your life, we never got round to it.

Magda We … er … we got sidetracked.

Kurt Yes, we did. So … tomorrow?

Magda Perhaps…

Kurt Maybe we could see a film?

Magda (*amazed*) They've got a picture house? Here?

Kurt Yes. This weekend they're showing *Top Hat* … wonderful film.

Magda You've seen it?

Kurt (*nodding*) And I'd love to see it again.

Magda (*smiling*) Fred Astaire and Ginger Rogers.

Kurt I can see that you're weakening.

Magda I'll have to think about it.

Kurt All right … You do that, I can wait… (*He pauses*) I wouldn't invade your privacy … You mustn't be frightened of me.

Magda I'm not frightened — of you.

*There is a pause and then Magda turns and walks quickly away and
we hear the screeching of the seagulls and the sound of the sea*

*In a moment Kurt returns to the bench and starts to sing the first few
lines of* Top Hat, *he might even dance a few steps as the Lights fade
to Black-out*

SCENE 3

The Lights come up on Hans who is standing behind the bench

Hans I've been seeing Mary nearly every day … apart from Sundays
when they all go to church … to mass … and then to Sunday school
… and then to evening service! Her mother insists … some kind of
religious fanatic. I wouldn't stand for it but her father's come home,
he's not well … so she feels she has to go. I don't like saying anything
but she needs my dad to talk to her … about religion… "the opium
of the people".

Pause

I watch her and the family leave for church … hide behind the bus
shelter … just to see her … you know. The last time we went to the
pictures we sat on the back row and I put my arm round her and she
kind of snuggled up … close … and I kissed her … properly … on
the lips … such soft lips … music from *Stage-Coach* thundered on
… it was fantastic. I can't stop thinking about her … all the time.

He looks down towards the harbour

She's painted the boat terracotta … didn't need much help. She
says that if her mother knew there'd be real trouble … so I go along
with it just to be with her. We met earlier, went for a walk but she

was quiet… I think it was because of the other night. (*He sits on the grass mound*) You see… I brought her up here … and … er … I got a bit carried away … you know … I overstepped the mark and she didn't respond. It made me feel guilty … but if I love her then there's nothing to be guilty about, is there?

Mary enters

Mary (*calling*) Hans.

Hans You're late.

Mary I know … there's just been the most awful row.

Hans What about?

Mary You. Mother's found out.

Hans How?

Mary John told her.

Hans I thought you'd sworn him to secrecy.

Mary I know but he's only seven. I should have thought … He can't tell a lie…

Hans Just our luck… (*He smiles*) Another George Washington?

Mary It's not funny. Well … he just can't … and at tea Mother asked if we'd both enjoyed the swim, before I could get a word in he said "Mary didn't go" — and then it all came out. I shouldn't be here, I had to check some homework with Celia, that was the excuse — so I'll have to be quick.

Hans I'm glad it has come out. I'm fed up with this cloak and dagger business, having to meet in secret, slipping into the pictures when it has all started. Let me meet your mother.

Mary No. That wouldn't help…

Hans Please. Let her see that I'm not a monster … Let me tell her about Dad — that he's not a Nazi — then everything would be all right.

Mary You don't know Mother — she can't be rational about such things, all she knows is that she's stranded here because of the war. You can't get away from it. Remember, only last week a woman internee threw herself off the cliffs … Just imagine being driven to do that … Mother couldn't talk about it. She didn't want to have a holiday here and now she's forced to live here. Try to understand.

There's a lot of resentment and bitterness: her cousin is missing since Dunkirk, my sister Kathleen's just joined the WRENs — James is about to be called up and any moment now Dad says the bombing will start. So don't you see as far as Mother's concerned the internees are all part of it — they are the enemy and they're here, and that, I'm afraid, includes you.

Hans But she lets John and Rita play with the German kids. I've seen them down on the beach.

Mary That's acceptable because they're just kids. For them the war isn't a reality — they've just got lots of new friends … They don't think of them as being "on the other side"— they don't really know what that means.

Hans Your mother thinks I'm on the other side — doesn't she? And she hasn't even met me. It's ridiculous. Don't you see? I was born in this country, Mother and Father lived and worked here for seventeen years. For a while Dad was a journalist for *The Times*, you can't get more English than that. But he didn't like the paper's politics, or rather they didn't like his politics, so he moved to the northern circuit. Anyway, I feel English — British — whatever that means — and I don't mean Elgar at the Free Trade Hall.

Mary looks at him

Pomp and Circumstance and all that. Like Dad I don't stay on at the pictures for *God Save The King* 'cos it's boring and pointless. But that doesn't make us any less English than you or your mother. (*He pauses*) I've told you my dad's not a Fascist, he nearly went to Spain, wanted to follow George Orwell, to fight against Franco, but Mother stopped him, they had such a fucking argument … Sorry, I shouldn't have used — er — that word.

Mary Is it blasphemous?

Hans No.

Mary Then what does it mean?

Hans It's a vulgar — crude word … It means …

Mary Yes?

Hans It means intercourse…

Mary Intercourse?
Hans Sexual intercourse.

Pause

I'm sorry. I've embarrassed you. Dad says that swear words can make a significant impact as long as they're not overused, otherwise they reveal a — a paucity of language. I've no excuse, I got carried away. Forgive me?

Mary Sometimes I don't know if it's you talking — or your father.

Hans So you don't think I've any ideas of my own?

Mary I don't know what I think. I only know that — that — I'm not going to be able to see you — any more.

Hans What?

Mary Mother's made me promise — a solemn promise, what we call "the Catholic hand of honour" — and it would be a sin for me to break it.

Hans I don't believe it. You're nearly seventeen — it's emotional blackmail. I won't go on about your church … I realize there's no point but at least stand up to your mother. (*He pauses*) For me?

Mary (*nearly in tears*) It's not as easy as that … you don't understand. I have to go … Don't make it difficult. Please?

Hans goes up to her and takes her in his arms

Hans Can you honestly say that you're happy with this? That you can agree to your mother's — absurd conditions?

Mary I have to.

Hans Now that your father's home — get him on your side.

Mary I can't … That's part of the trouble — he's too ill. So you see, Mother needs me — the others don't really understand, they're too young. My uncle's arranged a nurse to come over — to live in — she arrives today … It's as serious as that.

Hans I'm sorry… I want to help you…

Mary You can help me by letting me keep my promise.

Hans Promise! So at the end of the day— I don't count … It doesn't really have anything to do with your father.

Mary It does — more than I can say. Hans … You know — you know you count.

Hans Well, you've got a funny way of showing it. (*He releases his hold*) I think this is all to do with the other night — when we came up here.

Mary It was after curfew.

Hans So what? All right, it was dark. You could have made some excuse when you got home. You've become very good at making excuses.

Mary Telling lies …

Hans In order to meet me. Mary. It's only because I love you — that I wanted to — you know … I didn't mean to upset you. I just wanted to touch you — to be close to you. That's all …

Mary I was frightened …

Hans Of me?

Mary Of myself — and it would be a sin — a mortal sin.

Hans Your church has really got its tentacles round you, hasn't it? What do the Jesuits say? Give me a child until the age of seven and we've got him for life.

Mary moves away

Hans You're not the girl I fell in love with.

Mary Of course I am.

Hans Asking me to stop seeing you, how the hell can I …

Mary Listen. Just listen. It's not because of that night — believe me … It's for other reasons.

Hans What reasons?

Mary I can't tell you. Hans, do it for me? It would be a test — of your love.

Hans To give you up — would be the test? I can't believe I'm hearing this … The promises we made. (*Scathingly*) They didn't mean anything.

Mary You know that's not true …

A young woman's voice calling from the top path: "Mary… Mary…"

Mary That's Celia. I have to go.
Hans (*grabbing hold of her*) You can't — not like this …
Mary (*breaking from his hold*) I have to. And don't try to see me.
Hans I can't promise that.
Mary Please … and don't follow me…

Mary rushes off via the top path

Hans runs after her

Hans (*defiantly calling out*) I won't let you go — I won't, you know…
(*He turns round and paces towards the harbour*) I won't … Fuck
… fuck … fuck …

The seagulls respond loudly as the Lights fade to Black-out

Scene 4

The same. Evening

Kurt is alone, smoking

Kurt Magda kept me waiting for three days and then at last said "yes"
— to going to see *Top Hat*. First we had tea at Alandale's Cafe. (*He
smiles*) It was like being a teenager again — you know, on a first date.
The programme changes and whatever the film, we always go. I think
it makes us feel as if things are normal … We merge with the crowd
— forget that we're internees and — all the problems. For one thing
I've run out of money — they won't transfer cash from my London
account. Magda got some sewing jobs, dressmaking, etc., working
for an English family stranded here — and through her they've taken
me on as a part-time gardener! (*He laughs*) I'm getting very good at
it. My young room-mate is madly in love with the daughter of the
house, but she has been forbidden to meet him … Poor boy — he's
distraught — desperate.

There is a screeching of the seagulls, and Kurt stubs out his cheroot and looks at his watch

I've been seeing Magda nearly every day. We go for walks to Bradda Head, well as far as the barbed wire, and we meet here ... and sit ... and talk. (*He pauses*) She seems to enjoy it and yet she keeps a certain distance ... so I find it difficult, not really knowing how to ... er ... how do you say...? Play my hand.

Magda rushes in, distressed

Magda Kurt! Kurt!

Kurt turns round and, seeing her distress, goes to her

There's been an awful fight, well ... It started with the pro-Nazis insulting the Jews, (*with intensity*) they were vile, and it quickly got out of hand ... The leaders started to fight, no holds barred and we tried to intervene...

Kurt We?

Magda Lili and — er — some of our friends. It was hopeless — they were just too strong for us. Mrs Parker heard the din and called in the Commandant. She arrived with two policemen. There were harsh words. The threat of being put in prison and then she — gave us the usual platitudes about — learning to live together. We've heard it all before. Anyway, the outcome is that — some of us — are going to be moved, next door to the police station. Oh God, it was awful. (*She sits on the bench and lights a cigarette*)

The Lights slowly fade as dusk approaches during the following

Kurt Listen to me, Magda. You don't want your name on the trouble-makers list — there's enough to contend with without any additional — surveillance. Go and see the Commandant and talk to her.

Magda No, we'll be better off in another house and there'll be no need of surveillance because there won't be any more trouble, it will be all right — you'll see.

Kurt I hope so. (*He pauses*) Magda, you worry me.

Magda You shouldn't.

Kurt I can't help it.

Magda (*simply*) I'm not worth your concern… I'm not so important.

Kurt (*taking her hand*) You are to me.

Magda slightly moves her hand from his hold, but Hans does not let her withdraw

Kurt (*quietly*) I love you — you know I do.

Magda Oh, very charming. *Di vecchio stampa* — or rather should I say "old fashioned". Very Ronald Colman.

Kurt (*withdrawing his hold*) Why are you so cynical?

Magda Life has taught me — to be cynical.

Kurt Because someone let you down? …Very badly?

Magda (*rising and moving away*) Not someone … Shall we say "life" let me down — very badly.

Kurt Then isn't it time you allowed life to give you some — reassurance?

Magda Can't you understand, it's too late. Too late. Kurt, at your age … Well, you really should know better. (*She stubs out the cigarette with her shoe*)

Kurt You think I'm too old…? Dear God… I never thought of that — (*pronounced "dohf"*) *doof*, stupid, foolish man …

Magda No — of course you're not too old.

Kurt Then why are you putting me through all these — how do you say — er — hoops?

Magda Because I'm frightened.

Kurt You've said that before. What of?

Magda (*quietly*) Love.

Kurt goes to her, holds her, looks at her and they embrace. There is a moment of hesitation before Magda allows him to kiss her but when he does it is a long and passionate kiss

In the distance we can hear the siren

Magda Curfew.
Kurt (*sitting on the grass mound and holding her hands*) To hell with
    curfew… Oh, you silly girl…
Magda No, not a girl — a woman. Kurt — look at me…

*With both hands she firmly takes his head so that he is forced to look
at her face*

    Look at me — don't delude yourself…
Kurt Magda — don't put yourself down.

He draws her down on to the mound

    You're beautiful. (*He slowly starts to unbutton Magda's blouse*)
Magda Kurt?
Kurt Yes?
Magda Be gentle…

Pause

Kurt The first time?
Magda (*nodding*) The first time.
Kurt My darling.

*Kurt lies close to her and caresses her passionately. The sea crashes
on to the beach as the Lights slowly fade to Black-out*

SCENE 5

The same

*Mary is standing, looking out to sea. She is wearing her navy blue school
mackintosh and stockings with black shoes. She also wears a brimmed
school hat and is holding above her head a wet umbrella*

*Hans is standing on the upper cliff path and is wearing a dark grey suit
and a black tie and a dark, wet mackintosh. He is looking at Mary. After
a moment of what looks like a "still"*

Hans (*quietly*) Mary.
Mary (*turning with the sound of his voice*) Hans. It was good of you
to go — to church.
Hans I hate funerals … I kept thinking of Mother.
Mary I'm sorry.
Hans It's all right … Dad says we shouldn't be shielded from it …

Mary looks at him

From dying, from death. Anyway, I wanted to — and I wanted to
see you.

Pause. He looks at her umbrella

Mary. It has stopped raining.

Mary closes the umbrella

Mary When we came into church — I saw you — standing at the
back…
Hans I didn't recognize you.

Mary looks at him

The full school uniform … (*Roguishly*) I think it was the hat …

The tension is released through their laughter

Hans That's better.
Mary (*taking off the hat and putting it on the bench with the umbrella*)
I hate it! Always have.
Hans Vanity. In your church isn't that a sin?
Mary I don't want to talk about my church.
Hans Sorry.
Mary I don't think I believe in my church any more…
Hans Why?
Mary When Mother made me promise not to see you…

Hans The … The "Catholic hand of honour" bit?

Mary Yes. Well … I made another promise — which I couldn't tell you.

Hans To your mother?

Mary No. To God — that was the solemn promise, that if I didn't see you, then He would let Daddy live. He would answer my prayer.

Hans Well, if He exists, He didn't answer, not in the way you wanted.

Mary If He exists then He's a cruel God — and I can't believe in Him anymore.

Hans Well … it's a good start…

Mary To what?

Hans To becoming — a free thinker. (*He smiles*) But I think you need my dad to really put you through your paces.

Mary (*smiling*) Then ask him.

Hans You'll have to wait until the war's over.

Mary Then I'll wait.

They embrace and kiss

Hans I never stopped thinking about you.

Mary Me too. I might have lost you. And I do want to be — close to you — like the other night.

Hans And we're never going to lose each other … I mean — we might not be able to meet — but we'll never lose each other— (*he beats his fist against his heart*) not in here. The truth is … Mary, are you listening? They're taking me over to Douglas tomorrow.

Mary Tomorrow! Because you're seventeen?

Hans Well, not just that. Maybe they've decided that as the son of a "German spy" I might be responsible for passing on information. Who knows?

Mary Bastards!

Hans Mary! I never thought I'd hear you …

Mary Well, they are. I can't bear it … I can't … (*She is in tears*)

Hans (*holding her tenderly*) Sshh, sshh — don't cry…

Mary Which camp are you going to?

Hans Onchan Camp, Dad's camp …

Mary (*bravely*) At least you'll be together. Would I be able to see you — to visit you?

Hans It's an enclosed camp. But you will write to me, won't you?

Mary Of course. And you to me?

Hans The letters are censored.

Mary I don't mind the censor knowing how much I love you. Do you?

Hans Let's give him a thrill.

Pause

Mary I don't want you to go.

Hans I don't want to go. Parting isn't such sweet sorrow. Shakespeare got it wrong.

Mary But at least you'll be on the island.

Hans You could come over from school and walk past the camp.

Mary Yes. I could wave to you.

Hans I'll be on the lookout.

Mary About four-thirty. Promise?

Hans Promise …

They embrace again

Kurt enters from the top path

Kurt Hans. (*To Mary*) I'm sorry. (*To Hans*) They're looking for you … There's been a change of plan and they're taking you over to Douglas *now* … There's a van waiting … They say it's urgent.

Hans Why urgent?

Kurt How do I know? I tried to quiz them but — what do you say…? Oh yes — I got a flea in my ear. I promised I would get you.

Hans All right … just one minute.

Kurt (*solemnly*) One minute.

Kurt disappears out of sight

Hans puts his hands on Mary's shoulders

Hans Be brave. No tears.

Mary nods and then takes out of her pocket a small, painted, wooden model of her father's boat

Mary I hoped you'd be here. That's why I brought this … I asked James to make it — but I painted it — for your birthday. (*She hands it to him*) To remember.

Hans takes it and looks at it

Hans But I'm always going to remember. *The Glee Maiden.*

They both look down to the harbour, holding hands

And there she is. Isn't she beautiful?
Kurt (*off; urgently*) Hans. *Schnell* … quick… *quick*!

Hans and Mary turn to face each other

Hans I'll look out for you — weekdays — four-thirty.
Mary I'll be there.
Hans (*picking up her hat and umbrella*) Come — it's time. (*He takes her hand*)

As they start to go Mary suddenly stops

Mary Look … look … a rainbow.

Hans has his arms round her as they both look at the rainbow

Hans Fantastic.
Mary It's a lucky omen … for us.
Hans I love you. Come on! Come on!

They walk swiftly and happily up stage and as they disappear, the Lights cross-fade and Kurt is seen isolated in a spotlight

Kurt Hans only spent one night in Douglas. He was then taken with his father to Liverpool and the following day, July the first, they set sail for Canada, on the *Arandora Star*, an old cruise liner. On board were four hundred and seventy Germans and seven hundred and thirty Italians. So that the Germans would know that a ship carried prisoners of war the ship flew the swastika pennant below the red ensign. Nevertheless the *Arandora Star* was torpedoed on July the second. There were five hundred and eighty survivors. Hans and his father were not among them.

We hear the sound of the sea. Fade to Black-out

Scene 6

The same

Kurt is alone, waiting, tense and anxious

In a moment Magda enters from US

Magda Lili said you wanted to see me.

Pause

Kurt Yes. (*He takes a letter out of his pocket*) This came today. It was addressed to me. It's anonymous — from a well-wisher. (*He passes the letter to Magda*)

She starts to read it

Magda It didn't take them long, did it? The fight the other night ... Yes — I lied about it. (*She looks up from the letter*) They'd found out that five of us were of (*with mock German accent*) "the oldest profession

in the world". Oh, they loved it, "decadence, immorality" — such
self-righteous anger... (*She looks at the letter*) Yes ... well ... the rest
of this is a pack of lies. (*She screws up the letter and looks at Kurt*) If
you could see the expression on your face. So — judgemental.

Kurt I want you to tell me the truth.

Magda The truth. About what? About how I became (*with German
accent*) "a fallen woman"? Is that what you want to know? Haven't
you ever been with one? A man of your age — surely?

Kurt Please. Stop it. Magda — stop it ...

Magda You want to know why I didn't tell you. (*She laughs*) How
could I tell you? Don't be ridiculous. I just decided, and believe me
it wasn't easy, to avoid telling you the whole truth. I wasn't in the
witness box under oath.

Kurt I thought there was complete trust ... I believed in everything
you told me ... I accepted it as the truth.

Magda Then if the truth is so important I'll give you the truth. Where
shall I start? To put the record straight ... I was an invoice clerk — in
the dye house, not a secretary. Mother needed me, she wasn't well,
so I left, helped her run the dressmaking business — if you could
call it a business.

Kurt In St Anne's Square.

Magda In Salford ... We had to have the light on — all day. We worked
hard but nobody could afford new clothes ... They wouldn't take
me back at the mill, so what was there left to do? The dole? It was
pathetic. Means tests. Interviews. Visits to the pawn shop. Have you
the faintest idea what it was like? (*She pauses*) No, of course you
haven't ... Another world, my darling.

Kurt You said that your mother had been ill.

Magda She was — for a long time.

Kurt And you had looked after her.

Magda As best I could. Eventually they took her into hospital and
she was diagnosed with cancer — had to have an operation. They
discharged her — gave her six or seven months. They were going to
put her in the workhouse ... No way. I wanted her to be cared for, so
I put her in a posh home — run by nuns — starched sheets smelling
of lavender — trays with lace cloths — china cups. She'd had a hard
life, a bloody hard life, it was the least I could do. I kept her there until

she died. (*She smiles*) I haven't finished paying for the funeral but I don't think they'll catch up with me here. Do you? And then what happened? I was picked up in Piccadilly. By the police.

Kurt I just can't believe it. It seems that I fell in love with a person who doesn't exist … Lie after lie … You told me a — a fiction — which I accepted as the truth.

Magda It was the life that I wished I had lived! It was a chance to start again — a clean slate. Impossible to resist. Can't you understand that? I was being — respected, courted. I was a person in my own right, no longer a woman who — who had to please her customers …

Kurt My God, when I think that I was afraid to make any physical contact. I feared your rejection … No doubt you found that very amusing?

Magda I kept you at arm's length because — because I believed you were too good for me. An inner voice, my conscience if you like, told me that if I kept you at a distance, if I played the role of "the good woman", then I could hold on to you. Laughable, isn't it? But that was the contract I made with myself. Unfortunately I couldn't keep it … Emotions took over — and that made it quite different.

Kurt Are you saying that with your — "customers" there was no emotion?

Magda That's exactly what I'm saying. Like the letter, they were anonymous, they travelled incognito, that was how they wanted it, that was what they expected. Few words, if any, were spoken, I wasn't into any of the kinky business ——

Kurt Please … please…

Magda —that was always made very clear. Quite a prude, aren't you?

Kurt I loved you.

Magda Is it already the past tense? Yes. I believe you did. I knew — as soon as you kissed me. Well, you'll be pleased to know that we never kissed the customers — none of the girls did, that was the rule. So in spite of the *intimità*, the "intimacy", a kind of emotional distance was preserved and that, don't you see? … that was my protection. That was my—little—bit—of—dignity. It became — a rule of life.

Kurt A life that you chose to live.

Magda There was no choice — haven't I made that clear?

Silence

Kurt All right. You had to make a difficult decision, about your mother.

Magda Difficult … You have no idea — no idea…

Kurt Listen to me. I can identify with that decision. And I'm not being judgmental.

Magda Kurt, I don't want to be patronized.

Kurt I'm not patronizing you … dear God, how can I put it into words? The right words.

Magda Make the effort. I did.

Kurt In spite of everything you've said I … I can't — feel the same — now that I know. And, for the record, since you asked, I've never been with a prostitute. I've never paid for love — I mean sex. This may be difficult for you to believe — coming to London — working in the theatre …

Magda Go on.

Kurt You said that I was a prude — maybe I am. My youth, my — er — conditioning … Our Jewish faith was strong. One grew up to have — respect for a woman, both before and during marriage. Loyalty mattered, to the family, and it mustn't be sullied by scandal by behaviour that would bring shame or disgrace — that is how we were brought up. (*He pauses*) I was married — for a year — but she died at the end of the First War … She was a nurse. I never thought that I would fall in love again — but I did. I'm sorry that I am not big enough to say: Magda, it doesn't really matter. I wish that I could say it — but I can't… And I don't know if, in time, I would be able to think differently. Can you understand?

Magda I'll try, I have no pride, I'll be patient. We have a lot of time.

Kurt No, we don't. If we had, then we could put it to the test. I leave this afternoon. They're taking a few of us to Douglas. On the train.

Magda Why?

Kurt They've just realized that I'm only fifty-eight, a mere youngster, no longer eligible for the cushy life here in Port Erin.

Magda Which camp?

Kurt I don't know. Rumour has it that I might be sent overseas. I saw the Commandant and in so many words she made it clear that they are shipping a lot of the prisoners to the — er — Dominions … Marvellous word, isn't it?

Magda Sent overseas? Why?

Kurt Where I will be "safer", where I can't "corrupt" others. They've found out that I was a member of the Communist party. For God's sake one had to do something when the Nazis came into power. (*He looks at his watch*) It's time to go. I have to report to the Commandant's Office.

Magda rushes to him and puts her arms round him holding on to him passionately

Magda No… No … Please … Please…

Kurt slowly releases Magda's hold

Kurt At least now there's no deception.

Magda (*bravely trying to compose herself*) If they send you overseas, you'll write?

Kurt Yes… I'll write.

Magda I'll see your next show at the Opera House.

Kurt You do that.

Magda (*holding back the tears*) Yes … Yes… I'll look out for you.

Kurt nods and starts to go, then suddenly stops

Kurt You said — it was the first time — here — that's what you said. Remember?

Magda Oh yes, I remember — and it was.

Kurt How could it have been?

Magda Do I have to — spell — it — out?

Kurt (*after a pause; smiling*) No … And Magda?

Magda What?

Kurt Take care …
Magda I will. Kurt? Think of me.
Kurt I promise. *Auf Wiedersehen.*
Magda *Arrivederci.*

Kurt smiles and quickly exits by the lower cliff path

Magda focuses intently in his direction

Magda If he turns round… *If* he turns round … Dear God … Make him … Make him… (*In a moment, she turns away*) He didn't turn round. And it took ages before he was out of sight, and then I went bravely down to the station and waited … and waited — just in case I might see him. Ridiculous, isn't it? After nearly two hours the train came in and through the station fence I caught a glimpse of him. He didn't see me … I didn't want him to … and then the train pulled out of the station and I saw it disappear into the tunnel. (*She pauses*) I've thought about it a lot. He just needs time, time — to come to terms with it all. (*Resolutely*) And then he'll write. I know he will.

The Lights fade on Magda

Almost immediately Kurt is seen isolated in a spotlight wearing a smart cream macintosh

Kurt I was eventually shipped to Australia on the *Dunera*. It was built to carry two thousand men but on this trip she carried nearly three thousand. The voyage to Freemantle took nine weeks, an eternity. I lived in the hold, conditions were — disgraceful.

Pause

I was put in a special camp and then released in nineteen forty-two — no longer considered a "security risk"… (*He smiles*) After all, the Russians were now on our side! I've stayed in Australia, settled in Sydney and made a successful career.

Pause

I feel as though I belong here. At last I've got roots — a wife and a young family. I've never returned to England — there seemed to be no reason — to do so.

We hear the sound of the sea as the Lights fade to Black-out

SCENE 7

Mary is kneeling on the grass exactly as she was in Scene 1. She is wearing her school coat and is re-reading a short letter. In a moment she rises and looks way out to the sea

Magda enters wearing a thick coat and scarf

Magda I thought you'd be up here.

Mary (*smiling*) And you too?

Magda (*coming down to her side*) Well — it's difficult to keep away.

Mary Exactly.

Magda The sea's very rough.

Mary Yes. All those white horses.

Magda Have you had any news? A letter?

Mary It came this morning, he managed to get someone to post it — from Liverpool — just before he left. He said that he was being sent to Canada — on the same boat as his father.

Magda So soon. I'm sorry.

Mary I have to accept it. What else can I do? At least he'll be safe — away from the war. He says that he *will* write when he gets there.

Magda Of course he will. You'll have to be patient. Letters — letters can keep it alive.

Mary looks at her

The love.

Mary Yes. *Yes*, they have to.

Pause

Magda Did he say anything about Kurt? Has he seen him?

Mary He saw him briefly…

Magda And…?

Mary He says that Kurt thinks he's going to be sent overseas, but he doesn't know where.

Magda Does he mention — mention me?

Mary No. I thought Kurt would have written.

Magda No — no, he hasn't. We had an argument — a disagreement just before he left.

Mary I'm sorry— I'm sure that he'll write. He spent so much time with you.

Magda Yes, he did. He loved me.

Mary You know what the post is like. This one took five days.

Magda Yes. Yes. He'll write.

Mary (*smiling*) Every morning waiting for the postman to come. Such excitement — it's terrible…

Magda I know … You say to yourself every night: tomorrow … tomorrow will be the day.

Mary Yes, that's just how it is. (*She looks out to sea*) Oh, if only Ireland didn't exist.

Magda Why?

Mary Then I could look straight over there (*she points*) and there wouldn't be anything between me and Canada …

Magda Maybe they're on the same boat.

Mary looks at her

Kurt and Hans. Wouldn't that be lovely?

Mary I'd like that. (*She takes Magda's hand*) Close your eyes and make that wish … Right across the sea … Right across the ocean … It's telepathy, Magda … Whatever they're doing they'll think of us.

Magda Yes. All right, I will …

Mary Now, Magda … Now … *Now*…

They are both standing side by side holding hands and they close their eyes. The sea crashes on to the beach and we hear the screeching of the seagulls

In a moment the Lights slowly fade to Black-out

CURTAIN

FURNITURE AND PROPERTY LIST

Further dressing may be added at the director's discretion

Scene 1

On stage: Small, weather-beaten bench on old stone flags
Angled fence
Raised grass mound surrounded by pebbles
Remains of a fire

Set: Sketch book and pencil for **Mary**
Feather

Personal: **Hans**: bag of sweets, identity card

Scene 2

Set: Shopping basket. *In it*: thermos flask, cup, knitting bag with knitting

Personal: **Magda**: sunglasses
Kurt: wrist-watch (worn throughout), cheroot
Magda: wrist-watch (worn throughout)

Scene 3

No additional props required

Scene 4

Personal: **Kurt**: lighted cheroot
             Magda: cigarette, lighter

Scene 5

Off stage: Wet umbrella (**Mary**)

Personal: **Mary**: small model of boat

Scene 6

Personal: **Kurt**: letter

Scene 7

Set: Short letter for **Mary**

LIGHTING PLOT

Property fittings required: nil
Exterior. The same throughout

Scene 1

To open: General exterior daylight

Cue 1   **Hans**: "And she's called Mary!"   (Page 7)
            Fade quickly to black-out

Scene 2

To open: General exterior daylight

Cue 2   **Kurt** sings and might dance   (Page 14)
            Fade to black-out

Scene 3

To open: General exterior daylight

Cue 3   **Hans**: "Fuck … fuck … fuck…"   (Page 19)
            Fade to black-out

SCENE 4

To open: General exterior evening light

Cue 4	**Magda** lights a cigarette	(Page 20)
	Slowly fade to dusk lighting	
Cue 5	**Kurt** caresses **Magda**	(Page 22)
	Slowly fade to black-out	

SCENE 5

To open: General exterior daylight

Cue 6	**Mary**: "Look … look … a rainbow."	(Page 26)
	Rainbow effect	
Cue 7	**Mary** and **Hans** exit	(Page 27)
	Cross-fade to spot on **Kurt**	
Cue 8	**Kurt**: "…were not among them."	(Page 27)
	Fade to black-out	

SCENE 6

To open: General exterior daylight

Cue 9	**Magda**: "I know he will."	(Page 32)
	Cross-fade to spot on **Kurt**	
Cue 10	**Kurt**: "… no reason — to do so."	(Page 33)
	Fade to black-out	

Scene 7

To open: General exterior daylight

Cue 11   Sound of sea and seagulls   (Page 35)
                After a moment, slowly fade to black-out

EFFECTS PLOT

Printed by The Kingfisher Press, London NW10 7AS